Armenia
for Kids

Written by
Lisa Menasian Colloca

Illustrated by
US Illustrations

Apricot and Walnut Publishing, LLC

To my husband and our children

To my niece and nephews

To children of the Armenian Diaspora

Copyright © 2022 Lisa Colloca
All rights reserved. No part of this book may be reproduced or transmitted in any form or by any means, electronic or mechanical, including photocopying, recording, or by any information storage and retrieval system, without written permission from the author.

For information contact: Armeniaforkids@gmail.com

Library of Congress Control Number: 2022913542
ISBN 979-8-9866386-0-7 (hardcover)
ISBN 979-8-9866386-1-4 (softcover)

Published by Apricot and Walnut Publishing, LLC
Printed in the United States of America

Book Design: USIllustrations.com

Armeniaforkids.com

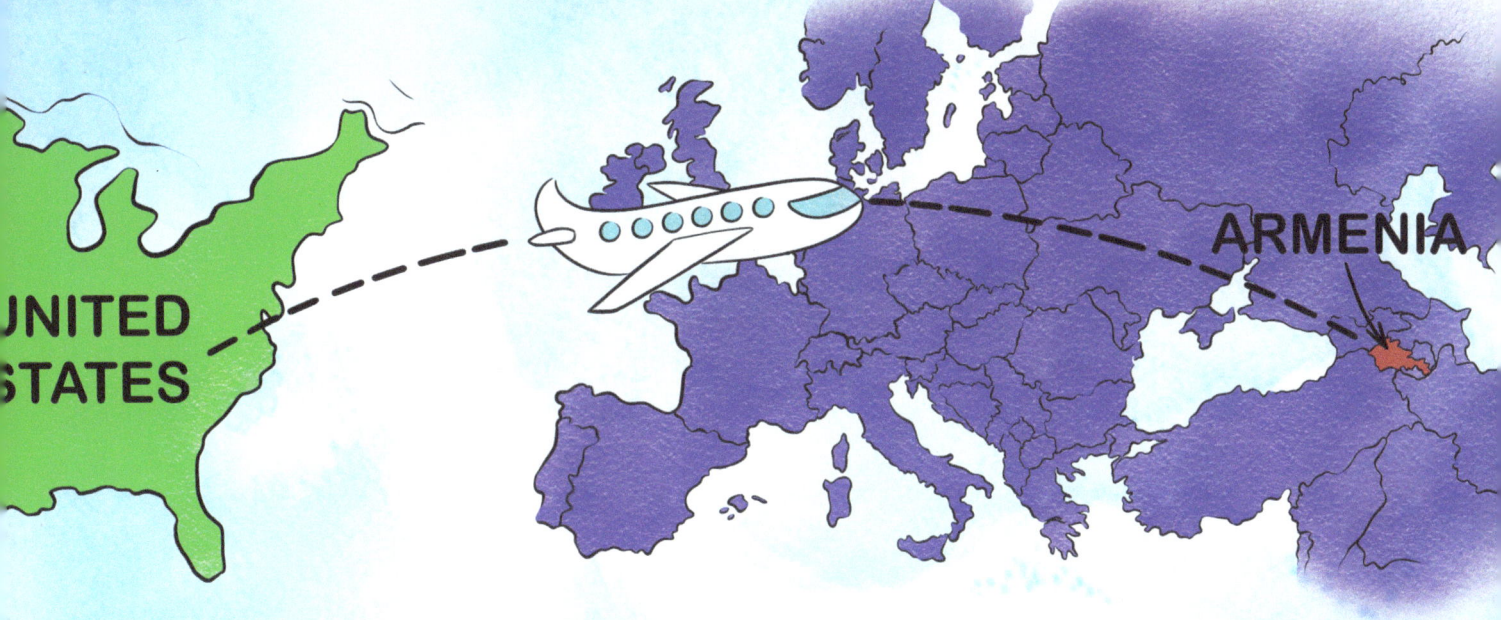

Table of Contents

Mt. Ararat/Khor Virap Monastery 4-5

Alphabet Park 6-7

Chess and Soccer 8-9

Geghard/Armenian Church Architecture 10-11

Lavash/Garni 12-13

Downtown Yerevan 14-15

Cascade/Traditional Dancing and Music 16-17

Vardavar/Family and Food 18-19

History Museum/Village 20-21

Lake Sevan/Dilijan 22-23

Armenian Genocide Memorial 24-25

Armenian Independence Day 26-27

Alphabet and Phrases 28-29

More About Armenia 30

About the Author 31

"Hi, I'm Talina, and this is my brother Mark. We're visiting Armenia! Come explore with us!"

"Wow, look at that—it's Mt. Ararat!" Mark said, eyeing the mountain rising before them. "The guidebook says Mt. Ararat is a symbol of strength for Armenians," Talina said. "It was part of historic Armenia and can be seen from far and wide." She turned to Mark, "We saw the mountain when we landed, remember?" "Yes," replied Mark who added, "It's actually a dormant (sleeping) volcano."

Did You Know?
Mt. Ararat is the biblical landing place of Noah's Ark.

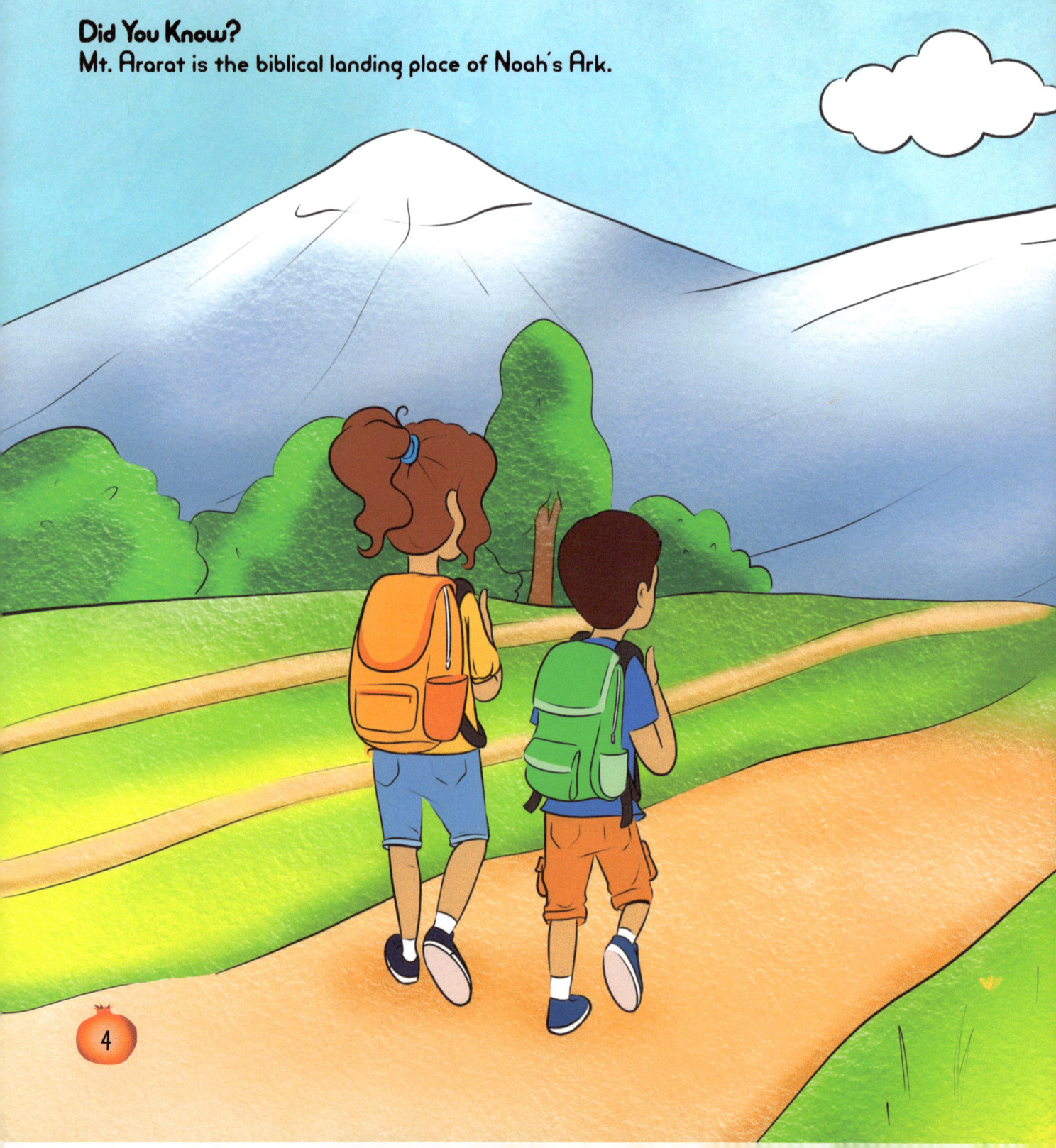

"Hey," Talina pointed. "There's Khor Virap Monastery at the foot of Mt. Ararat. The guidebook says that a long time ago, the Armenian King Trdat sent a Christian man named Gregory to live in a pit of poisonous snakes. Gregory survived and credited his faith in God. Years later Trdat called upon Gregory when the king fell ill. The king was cured and declared Armenia a Christian nation. Gregory became known as St. Gregory the Illuminator for bringing 'Light' to Armenia."

Did you know?
Armenia converted to Christianity in 301 A.D., making it the first Christian nation.

The next day, the children visited a local school and joined them on a field trip to the Alphabet Park.
"Woah, look at those letters—they're huge!" Mark exclaimed.
The teacher explained, "The stone Alphabet Park opened in 2005 in celebration of the 1600th birthday of the Armenian alphabet.* Mesrob Mashtotz developed the Armenian alphabet when he wrote down what he saw in a vision."

"Here's 'T' for my name," Talina said enthusiastically. "Where's 'M'?" Mark asked. "Over there," the teacher pointed. "Say 'banir!'" ('cheese!')

Did you know?
Three letters were added in the 12th century to make 38 in all – 31 consonants and seven vowels.

*Turn to p. 28 for the complete Armenian alphabet.

The next day, the children were invited to a chess class.
"Shakh yev mat!" ('Check mate!') Mark exclaimed.
"Good move," the teacher praised.
Armenia has many international champions. Chess may be a game of strategy and discipline, but for most it's a fun, national pastime.

Did You know?
In Armenia, Chess is a class in school, like Math and Reading.

After school, the pair joined their friends at fütbol (soccer) practice.
"Try to kick it past me," Talina challenged her brother.
They played until Mark said, "I'm hungry, let's get some lehmejun (pizza)."
"Great idea," Talina agreed.

Did You know?
Futbol is the most popular sport in Armenia but many other sports, such as basketball, gymnastics, volleyball, and hockey are also widely played.

This morning, the children ventured off to visit Geghard Monastery, a short ride from Yerevan, the capital. "Welcome," a priest greeted them, as a choir echoed inside. "Incredibly, Geghard was built into a mountainside from the 4th to the 13th centuries," he explained. "There are caves, wall carvings, and a spring runs beneath it. Relics—items of religious importance, were once hidden here." "Wow!" Mark said. "Indeed," said the priest.

"All are welcome to visit any of the nearly 4,000 churches and monasteries in Armenia. The stone architecture has a cross floor layout, vaulted ceilings, and a cone octagon dome. You may light a candle and say a prayer," he said.

"Monasteries were also places to learn science, math, philosophy, and languages," he added. "Perhaps you will visit Etchmiadzin Cathedral, or Saghmosavank, Haghartsin, Noravank, or Tatev Monasteries."

Did you Know?
Tatev Monastery, near the border of Iran, can be visited by taking the 'Wings of Tatev,' the world's longest reversible tram.

After leaving Geghard, the children stopped at a bakery on their way to nearby Garni.
"Here," the baker said, offering them a piece of lavash bread.
"Lavash is a strong, thin, stretchy bread made from a special yeast," the woman explained. "The dough is baked in a tonir (clay oven in the ground) by slapping it to the inside walls, then it is removed and cooled on a stone."
"Mmm, thank you," Mark said. "It's delicious," added Talina.

Did you know?
Lavash is a cultural tradition and is served with most meals.

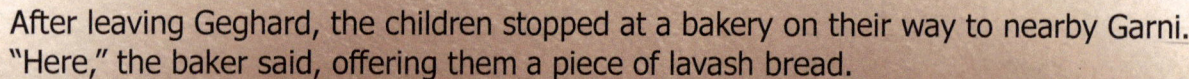

"What's Garni?" Mark asked.

She checked her guidebook. "Garni is an outdoor museum and the only Greco-Roman structure in the country. It was likely built for the sun god Mihr, but people aren't exactly sure what it was used for. Today it is the setting for celebrations and concerts."

Did you know?
The Ionic Greek columns at Garni are tall and thin, with decorative scrolls.

The next morning the two set out on foot to explore downtown Yerevan.
"Yerevan is known as the 'Pink City' for the pinkish volcanic tuff stone buildings that seem to glow at sunset," Talina read while Mark spun around, looking at the buildings. "Yerevan is a lively city with Republic Square in the center. Roads lead outward from the square like a web. The popular Northern Avenue is lined with clothing stores, restaurants, shops selling sweet treats, street vendors, musicians, and even people dancing in celebration. Dine at an outdoor café, play in the park, or see a performance at the Opera House."

Did you know?
At one time, Armenia held the record for making the world's largest chocolate bar. It was 224 ft. long and weighed 9,702 lbs!

The next afternoon, the two visited the Cascade—sets of stairs connecting art galleries. Outside, a friend spotted them. "Come dance!" he shouted, tossing them Armenian taraz (traditional dress).

"This is so much fun! I like the way my dress twirls," Talina said, spinning about.

"I want to learn to dance like them," Mark said of the young men.

In traditional Armenian dance, people often form an open circle or line and are connected by holding hands, linking pinky fingers, or waving hands in the air. Folk music is played on a dohl (a drum played with the hands), a duduk (similar to a recorder), and a kanun (a flat stringed instrument played on the lap).

Did you know?
Traditional Armenian festivals can be found in the United States and around the world.

The next day, they opened their door to a loud SPLASH!
"It's Vardavar!" a little boy yelled.
"I know about this!" Mark exclaimed. "It's held each summer, fourteen weeks after Easter, when people are allowed to splash water on absolutely *anyone*—even parents and teachers!"

Did you know?
Vardavar began in ancient times to honor the goddess of water, beauty, and love, Astgik. But today it is a church holiday and being sprinkled (or doused!) with water is considered a blessing.

That night, their friends greeted them with a bachig (kiss) on both cheeks. "Please, sit down. We have fish, shish kebab (skewered lamb) and chicken kebab, dolma (stuffed grape leaves), tomato and cucumber salad, jajuk (chilled cucumber yogurt) and, of course, lavash and hummus," their host explained. "For dessert, we have fresh fruit and gata, a round dough filled with nuts, cinnamon, and nutmeg."
"Mmm, everything looks and smells delicious!" Mark said and Talina agreed.

Did you know?
Armenian families are known for their generosity and for being warm and close-knit.

As they wandered back through Republic Square, the children eyed the History Museum of Armenia. A guide greeted them as they entered.
"This museum is home to many artifacts—items of historic or cultural importance," the guide explained. "To the left is a khachkar, a hand-chiseled cross stone, used to mark an important event or place. Learning this trade is often passed from father to son. And here is a bronze heliocentric (sun-centered) solar system from about 11 B.C. You see, the Armenian people knew the earth was round a long time ago."
"Is that an old shoe!?" Mark asked.
"Yes, in fact, it's the world's oldest shoe! It's 5,500 years old and made of leather. It was discovered in a cave," the guide responded.

Did you know?
Khachkars are like snowflakes-no two are exactly alike.

"The rich soil, mountain spring water, and sunny climate help grow delicious fruits like apricots, pomegranates, apples, peaches, and plums," the farmer explained.
"May I help pick some fruit?" Talina asked. "May I help sheer the sheep?" Mark asked.
"Of course," replied the farmer.
"What do you do with the sheep's wool?" asked Mark.
"The wool is cleaned, dipped in natural dyes, and dried before it is woven into strands for cloth, the farmer demonstrated. It is sometimes used for traditional crafts such as carpet weaving and needle lace."

Did you know?
The pomegranate is a symbol of prosperity, or a good harvest.

The next morning the two headed to Lake Sevan. "It's hot—let's cool off!" Talina suggested.

Lake Sevan is one of the world's largest freshwater lakes, and a popular vacation spot in the summer. When they were done swimming, the children headed to Dilijan for lunch. Nicknamed 'Little Switzerland' for its chalet-style buildings and forests, it's also known for its artists workshops and spas.

After lunch, they grabbed their backpacks and took a short hike on a path through the forests of Dilijan National Park. "I see the trail marker at the bridge up ahead," spied Mark. "And I see it on the map," said Talina.

Apple, walnut, willow, oak, beech and maple trees, along with gooseberry bushes, grow here. And animals such as deer, bear, and wolves live in this park.

Did you know?
The mineral-rich waters of Dilijan are known to heal some health problems.

Wanting to learn about their connection to the past, the children visited the Armenian Genocide Memorial and Museum.
There, the museum guide told them, "In 1915, during World War I, the Ottoman Empire, ruled by the Young Turks, wanted to erase the whole country of Armenia, and many, many people died. It was very tragic, but Armenians never lost hope."
Talina said, "That's awful." Mark added, "It is. It is also a reason why there are Armenians all around the world—like us."

On their last day, the children celebrated Armenian Independence Day in Republic Square.
"This looks a lot like America's Independence Day," Mark observed, as people sang the national anthem, 'Mer Hayrenik' ('Our Fatherland')."
Talina read from the guidebook, "The red stripe on the flag represents the nation's struggles, Christian faith, and freedom; the blue is for nature and peaceful skies; and the orange is for hard-working and creative people."
"We hope you enjoyed exploring Armenia as much as we did!" they said in unison.

Did you know?
Armenia was part of the Soviet Union until independence on September 21, 1991.

The Armenian Alphabet

Աա	Բբ	Գգ	Դդ	Եե	Զզ	Էէ	Ըը	Թթ
ayb	ben	gem	da	yech	za	eh	aht	to
ah	*buh*	*guh*	*duh*	*yeh*	*zuh*	*eh*	*uh*	*tuh*

Ժժ	Իի	Լլ	Խխ	Ծծ	Կկ	Հհ	Ձձ	Ղղ
zhe	ene	lyon	xeh	cah	ken	ho	dja	ghad
zh	*e*	*l*	*kh*	*ts*	*k*	*h*	*dz*	*rgh*

Ճճ	Մմ	Յյ	Նն	Շշ	Ոո	Չչ	Պպ	Ջջ
cheh	men	yi	new	sha	voh	cha	beh	jheh
ch/j	*m*	*y, h*	*n*	*sh*	*vo*	*ch*	*b/p*	*jo*

Ռռ	Սս	Վվ	Տտ	Րր	Ցց	Իւ	Փփ	Քք
ra	seh	vew	tyon	reh	tso	hyon	piyr	keh
r	*s*	*v*	*t*	*r*	*ts*	*u*	*p*	*k'*

Օօ	Ֆֆ
oh	feh
o	*f*

Armenian Phrases

Hi/Hello – **Bar-ev**
How are you? – **Inch-bes-es** or **Von-cek**
I am well – **Yes lav-em**
My name is _____ – **Im anu-nae** _____
What is your name? – **Inch-e-kvo-anune?**

I am _____ years old. – **Yes** _____ **tarekan yem.**
    1 – **mek**
    2 – **yerguk**
    3 – **yereq**
    4 – **chors**
    5 – **hing**
    6 – **vets**
    7 – **yoot**
    8 – **oot**
    9 – **inna**
    10 – **dasa**

Yes/No – **Ayo/Votsch**
Goodbye – **Ts-tes-ut-yun**
Please – **Khn-trem**
Thank you – **Shnor-rha-gal-yu-tuyn**
I love you – **Yes kez sirum em**
Mother/Father – **Mayr/Hayr**
Grandmother – **Mens mayr** or **Tatik**
Grandfather – **Mens hayr** or **Papik**
Sister/Brother – **K'yur/Yeghbayr**
Cousin – **Zar-mik** (male) **Zarmu-hi** (female)
Friend – **Un-ker**
Armenian/Armenia – **Hye/Hayastan**

More About Armenia

Pomegranates, Mt. Ararat, and khachkars are a few symbols that can be found throughout Armenia. An ancient nation steeped in history and rich cultural traditions, Armenia is a mountainous, landlocked Eurasian country bordered by Turkey, Georgia, Azerbaijan, and Iran. At one time, Armenia stretched from the Caspian Sea to the Black Sea, but now it is a little smaller than Belgium due to centuries of invasions. Its conversion to Christianity (301 A.D.) and the development of the Armenian language, (405 A.D.), are two reasons why Armenian culture has endured.

Today, the Republic of Armenia is a free, democratic nation with elected representatives and a Constitution. The Armenian Apostolic Church is the national church, and there is freedom of religion. There are two Armenian dialects—Eastern Armenian, largely spoken in Armenia, and Western Armenian, largely spoken outside of Armenia.

Yerevan, Armenia's capital, is a bustling, modern, European-style city with lots of people, vehicles, shops, restaurants, museums, theaters, entertainment complexes, art centers, and parks. There are many businesses, schools and universities as education is highly valued. Gyumi, Vanadzor, Vargharshapat, Tsaghkadzor, and Dilijan are the names of a few cities. There are also many towns and towns where people live traditionally, growing food and raising livestock. The land consists of mountains, valleys, forests, rivers, and fertile soil. The four seasons include hot, humid summers and cold, snowy winters.

Armenia has adopted a lot of traditions from European and Arab cultures including food, music, dancing, and art. Armenians pride themselves in having close-knit families and generous hospitality. There are about three million people living in Armenia and millions more living in the Diaspora (outside Armenia), including at least 1.5 million Armenians living in the United States.

Despite its unsettled history, Armenia continues to adapt and modernize, particularly in its growing technology sectors. Armenia has close relations with many western European nations such as France and Italy. Armenia also maintains security and economic ties with Russia as it continues to define itself independently on the world's political and economic stage.

To learn more, visit ArmeniaforKids.com

Acknowledgments

Thank you to my husband, Bob Colloca, for his love, friendship, and encouragement. You are an amazing husband and father; I treasure our trips to Armenia and the reason that led us there. Thank you to my parents, Mel and Judy Menasian for their love and support. I'm grateful for the church pilgrimage we took in 2009, my first trip to Armenia.

A special thank you to our children, Talina and Mark, for readily sharing thoughts and opinions on the manuscript and ideas for illustrations. You are the 'light of our family' and we are blessed to have you. Thank you to US Illustrations for turning my vision into reality with beautifully illustrated page spreads. Thank you to Laura Gaboudian for her early input and edits, and to Brooke Vitale, my copy editor. Thank you to Nancy Shields for your candid opinions.

A special thank you to my young beta-readers for their candid, invaluable insights: Anya Kakkad, Maya Kakkad, Kayla Kakkad, Grace Kanayan, Narek Kesablyan, Drew Menasian, Jax Menasian, Arthur Odabashian, Shant Odabashian, Hailey Shields, and Dylan Shields. You are the bright future!

About the Author

Lisa Menasian Colloca has a master's degree in history from Boston College and teaches advanced placement history in an urban high school in Massachusetts. A grandchild of Armenian Genocide survivors, she has had the privilege of traveling to Armenia on several occasions. Lisa began writing during the pandemic, as a gift to her children, which soon turned into a more serious venture. **Armenia for Kids** is a book she looked for when she was growing up but was unable to find. Lisa lives outside Boston with her husband and their two children.

www.ingramcontent.com/pod-product-compliance
Lightning Source LLC
Chambersburg PA
CBHW040725060526
44119CB00083B/325